D1283629

THEATER MAGIC

THEATER MAGIC

Behind the Scenes at a Children's Theater

by Cheryl Walsh Bellville

Carolrhoda Books, Inc./Minneapolis

The author would like to thank Ceil Victor and Gene Buck for their help and encouragement, and all the people at the Minneapolis Children's Theatre Company. Thank you also to Carol and Sonja Kostich for rearranging their busy lives to accommodate the preparation of this book.

LIBRARY OF CONGRESS CATALOGING-IN-PUBLICATION DATA

Bellville, Cheryl Walsh.
    Theater magic.

    Summary: Follows the Children's Theatre Company as it produces an adaptation of Hans Christian Andersen's "The Nightingale," describing how the play is planned, designed, cast, and rehearsed for its opening.
    1. Children's play—Presentation, etc.—Juvenile literature. [1. Plays—Production and direction. 2. Children's Theatre Company (Minneapolis, Minn.) 3. Fairy tales] I. Title.
PN3157.B35   1986   792'.0226   86-9757
ISBN 0-87614-278-1 (lib. bdg.)

1 2 3 4 5 6 7 8 9 10 96 95 94 93 92 91 90 89 88 87 86

For Susan and Ceil

This book is about a play called *The Nightingale*, performed by the Children's Theatre Company of Minneapolis, Minnesota. It is based on a story by Hans Christian Andersen.

A play is like magic. When you leave the familiar world outside and enter a dimly lit theater, you can let your imagination go and become part of a story from any time and place. You can become part of the magic of the theater.

6

The Story of the Nightingale

Long ago, China was ruled by emperors. The story of the nightingale takes place during such a time, in the city where the emperor lived. Travelers to this city were charmed by its beauty and by the emperor's palace, but what delighted them most was the song of the nightingale, a little gray bird that lived outside the city. When the emperor heard of this little bird, he sent a young girl who worked in his kitchen, along with members of his court, to find the bird and bring it back to the palace. The kitchen maid found the nightingale and asked the small bird to return with her. She returned to the palace with the nightingale, whose song pleased the emperor so much that the little bird was ordered to stay in the palace and sing forever.

One day, a mechanical nightingale made of gold and jewels arrived at the court as a gift from the emperor of Japan. The real nightingale was forgotten, and she flew back to the forest from which she had come. Meanwhile, the jeweled bird broke, and the emperor became very ill. The real nightingale learned of the emperor's illness and returned to the palace to sing him back to health. She then agreed that if she were allowed to sing for the other people of the land, as well as for the emperor, she would come often to the court and offer her gift of song.

Suddenly the house lights dim, and the audience grows quiet. The curtain rises on a single figure, a little girl. She introduces herself as Wu Ling, humble servant of the emperor of China, and the performance begins.

What is it that leads up to this magical moment? How are all of the wonderful illusions created? Who are the people working behind the scenes? This is the story of how this performance of *The Nightingale* was created, of how the people backstage and the people onstage joined together to create theater magic.

The idea for this play came from a book of the nightingale story illustrated by Nancy Ekholm Burkert. Ms. Burkert agreed to design the sets and costumes for the play, which were based on her illustrations. These illustrations place the story of the nightingale in the twelfth century.

Ms. Burkert's many drawings were used as patterns and guides by the people who made the backgrounds and sets (the scenes used in a play) and by those who made the properties, or props (objects used by the actors in a play), and costumes.

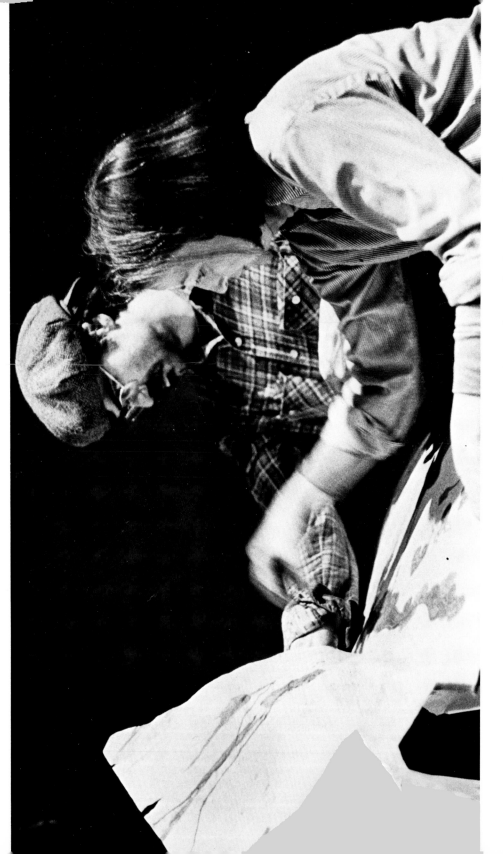

The creation of *The Nightingale* began with production meetings. At these meetings, the playwright (a person who writes plays or adapts the words of a story to play form), the composers (people who write music), the director (whose job it is to guide and teach the actors how to act out the script onstage), the costume and set designer (Nancy Burkert), and the heads of the scene, prop, and costume shops got together and decided how to turn the story into a play.

People who perform a play onstage are called actors and actresses. The Children's Theatre Company has an acting company, a group of people who regularly act in plays for this theater. When this play was being performed, the theater also had a school for the performing arts. Students from the school auditioned, or tried out, for parts in plays performed by the Children's Theatre. Four girls from the school were chosen to be members of the royal court for this play. One girl, Sonja, was chosen from outside the school to play the role of the emperor's kitchen maid.

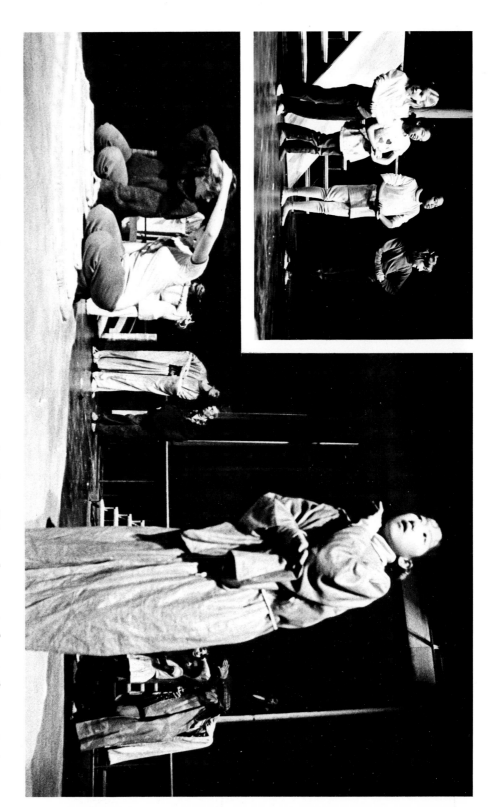

11

When actors practice their speaking parts and movements onstage, it is called rehearsing. At first, only small pieces of the play were rehearsed at one time. But as time went on, larger segments were prac-

ticed until whole scenes (parts of a play in which the action remains in one place) were rehearsed. By the end of rehearsals, the entire play was being practiced from beginning to end.

12

During the time in which rehearsals took place, the actors memorized their lines, learned cues (signals that tell them it is time to say or do something onstage), and studied their blocking. Blocking is the timing and placement for action on the stage.

Because this was an original production, one that had not been performed before, it was possible to make changes in the roles during rehearsals. Actors often evolve, or develop and refine, their roles throughout the entire time a play is being performed.

14

The younger actors and actresses, like Sonja, sometimes needed help finding ways to develop the characters they were playing.

For this kind of guidance, they looked to the more experienced actors as well as to the director.

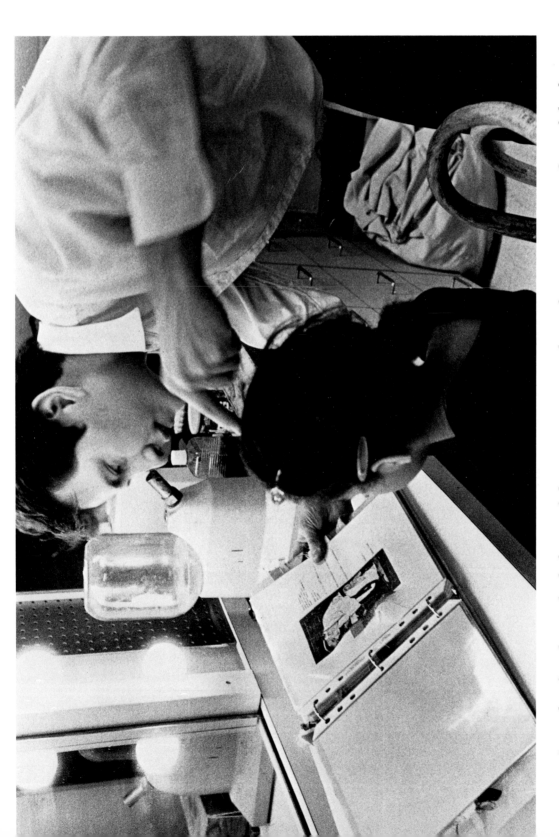

In order for the make-believe of the theater to seem real, the actors in this play had to look Chinese. Because almost all of them were Caucasian, changes had to be made in their appearance. One of the biggest changes was in their hairstyles. Since almost everyone in the play had to wear a wig, wigmakers had a big job ahead of them.

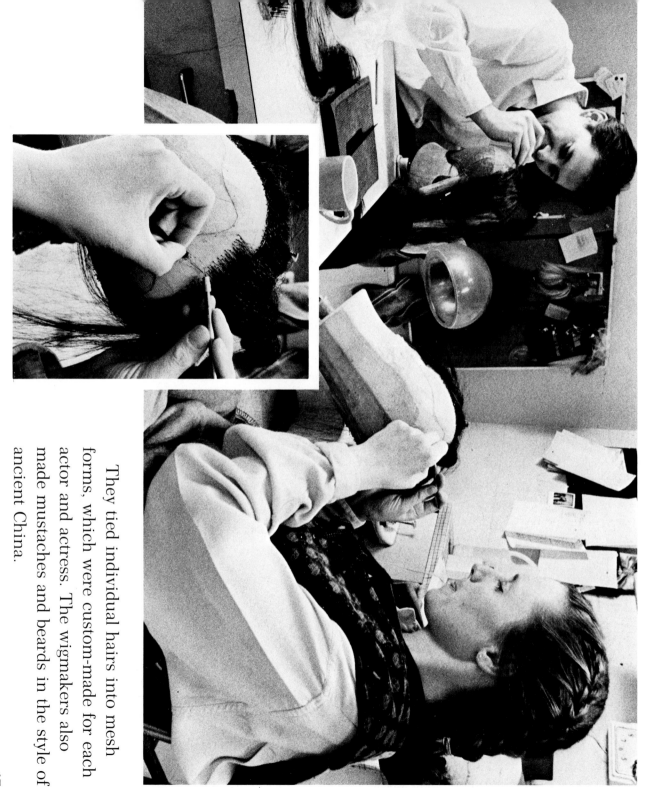

They tied individual hairs into mesh forms, which were custom-made for each actor and actress. The wigmakers also made mustaches and beards in the style of ancient China.

17

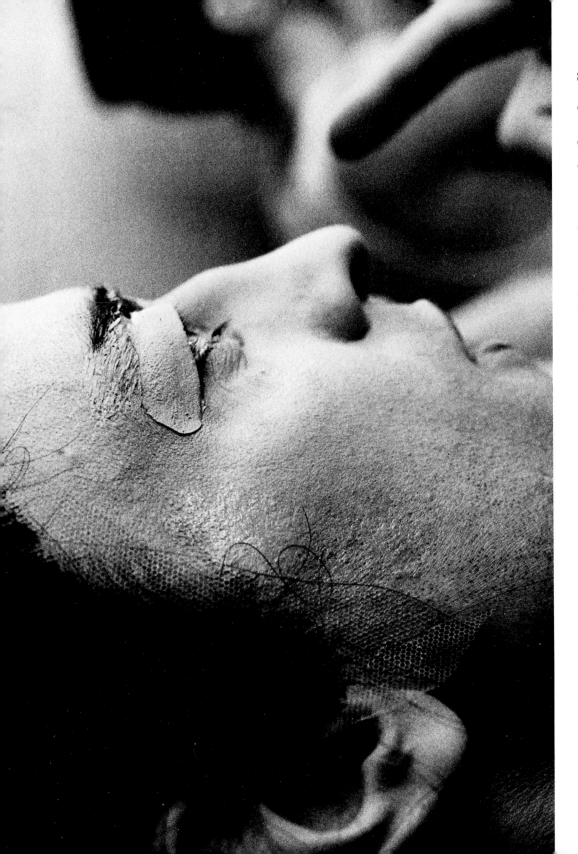

Another physical difference between the Western actors and their Asian roles was the shape of their eyelids. Artificial eyelids were made of rubber to fit each actor and actress.

These eyelids were then applied with adhesive before every dress rehearsal (rehearsals done in full costume) and performance.

18

Another way to help create illusion in the theater is with makeup. People on a stage wear makeup to emphasize their eyes and other features so that they can be seen easily from a distance. A makeup man

taught the cast (the entire group of people who perform onstage) how to apply makeup so that they would look Chinese. Eventually, the actors learned how to put on their own makeup.

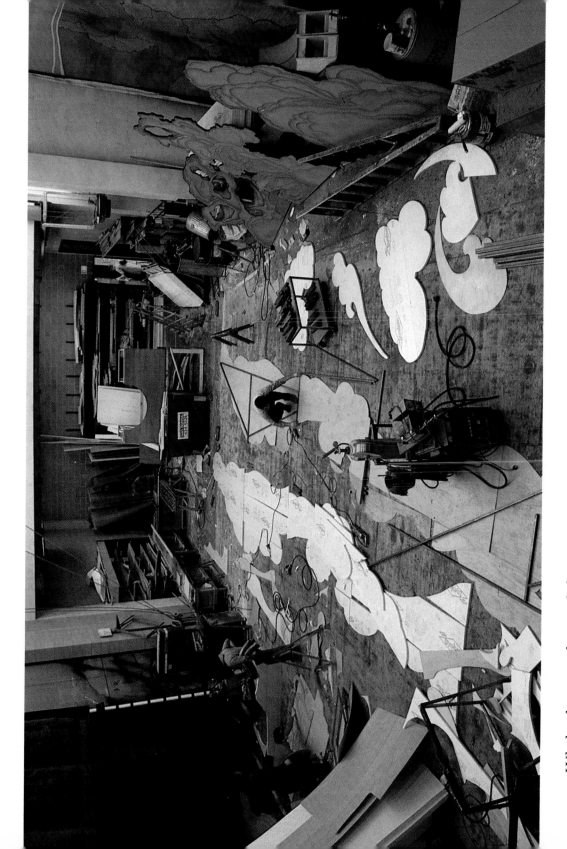

While the members of the cast were busy learning their parts and rehearsing, designers, builders, and costumers were working on other elements of the play in the different shops. Shops are work areas in which scenery and props are built, or where costumes are made.

The people in the shops used Ms. Burkert's drawings as guides for their work. These drawings were based on a careful study of Chinese life during the twelfth century.

Other books and illustrations were also used to get different ideas and to check for historical accuracy.

In the costume shop, mock, or imitation, costumes were cut out of muslin (a plain, cotton fabric) and sewn together. These muslin costumes were then used as patterns for the final costumes. The final costumes were made from fabrics similar to those worn in China in the twelfth century.

23

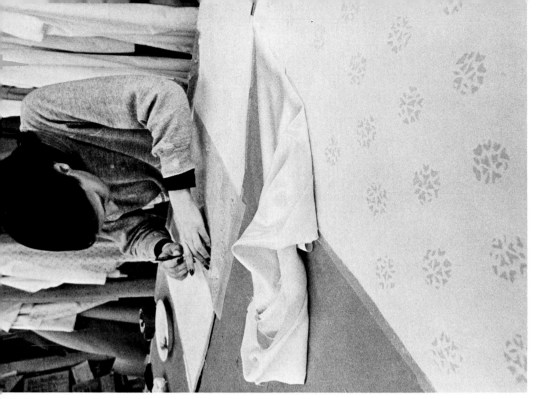

The designs on the fabrics were copied from ancient Chinese fabrics and printed by hand onto the cloth. When the muslin clothing looked just right, sewing began on the real costumes.

While the costumes were being made, each actor and actress had several fittings so that each article of clothing would fit perfectly.

Shoes, jewelry, hats, and other details for the costumes were also made in the costume shop.

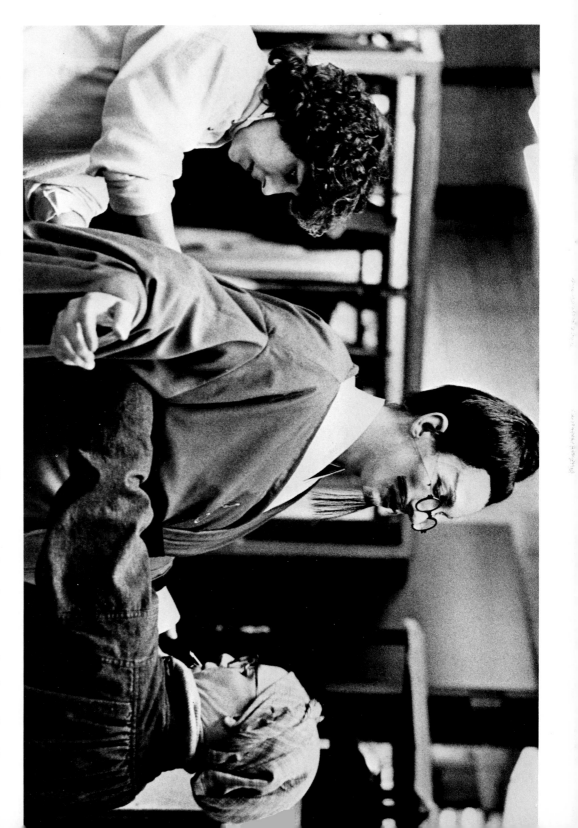

25

In order to attract an audience, a theater must let the public know when the play will be performed and a little about the play itself. For this reason, a photo call is usually arranged. Photographs of interesting aspects of the play are taken and then sent to newspapers and used on posters and other printed material to spread information about the play.

The emperor's costume and wig, the kitchen maid's costume, and one of the puppets that represented the nightingale were all finished early so that they could be used in the photo call.

One of the very special elements of this play was the use of puppets to represent the nightingale. Several puppets were designed to make different movements and to be used in different scenes in the play. For example, one puppet was designed to be held and moved by an actor onstage. Another night-ingale puppet did not move but was fastened to the end of a long beribboned pole, which was carried across the stage to represent flight. Yet another of the puppets sat on a perch and contained a very complex system of wires. When operated, this puppet could open and close its beak and flap its wings.

The first step in the construction of the more complex puppets was to sculpt the body of the bird in clay. A plaster mold was made from the clay model, and the mold was filled with foam rubber. The foam-rubber model was then baked to solidify the rubber.

29

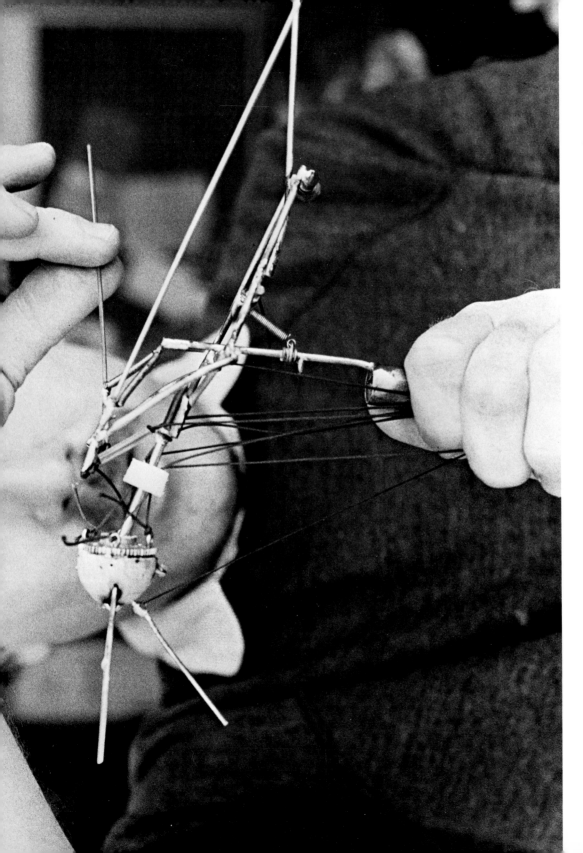

Metal skeletons, called armatures, were placed inside the rubber birds. Parts of the puppets could then be moved when the wires and strings that were attached to the armatures were pulled by the person operating the puppet. To the people in the audience, this would look like the movements of a real bird.

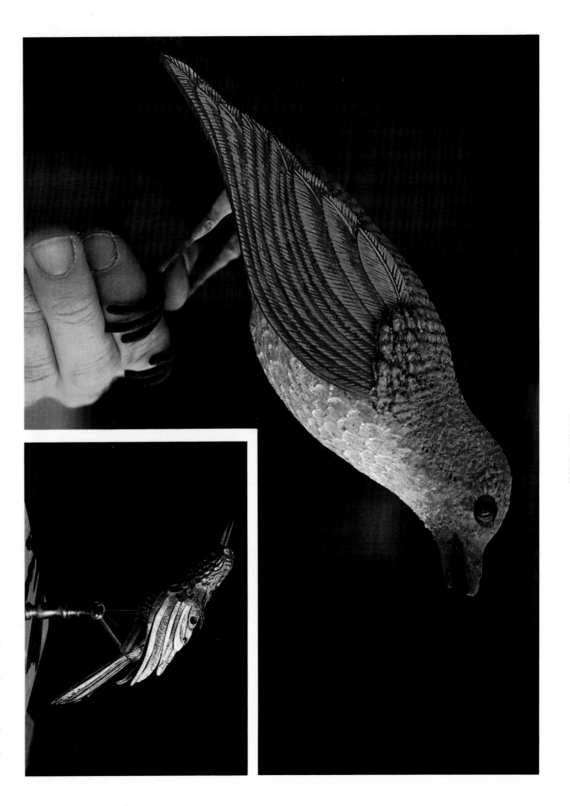

The finished foam-rubber birds were painted by hand to make them look like real nightingales.

There were also two puppets made to represent the mechanical nightingale that temporarily replaced the real bird in the affections of the emperor and his court.

In the scene shop, the largest structure in the play—the emperor's palace—was being built. It was so big that much of the work on it was done on the stage itself. Huge doors between the stage and the

scene shop allowed the palace to be moved in and out of the shop area when necessary.

The palace began as an elevated wooden floor with wooden supports for the roof.

As work progressed on the palace, cardboard tubes were placed over the wooden supports and then painted so that they resembled columns. Decorative touches were added day by day until the structure resembled a royal building of long-ago China.

35

Other parts of the sets were the back-drops (large pieces of cloth that are painted with scenery and hung at the rear of the stage) and the flats (flat pieces of scenery that are placed on the stage). The drawings that were used as guides for the backdrops

were carefully duplicated on the large pieces of cloth. The backdrops were so big that they had to be raised and lowered mechanically so the shop artist could reach different areas with her paint sprayer.

36

The flats were cut out of plywood with power saws, and supports were welded onto them so that they would stand upright.

In this play, flats were painted to resemble plants and shrubs and then placed around the palace. From the front, they created the illusion of three-dimensional objects, even though they were flat pieces.

The apron, or front, of the stage was built up with layers of plywood and foam and painted to resemble rocks and a stream flowing into a pool in front of the palace.

This added some actual depth to the scenery and contributed to the overall illusion of landscape on the stage.

39

This traditional theater is called a proscenium theater, one in which an arch separates the audience from the stage. The audience can see only what happens inside the frame of the proscenium arch. The actors and the stage crew (the people who move the sets and props for the various scenes) can hide above or to the sides of the arch to wait their turn to appear onstage or to create special effects.

40

Many special effects in this play were created by the sound and lighting technicians. Their work was done in booths that overlook the stage. These booths are located at the back of the house (the area in which the audience sits). The technicians watched

the rehearsals and performances from their booths. They worked with scripts that told them when to bring in or change the many lighting and sound effects so that they would blend together with the other parts of the play.

41

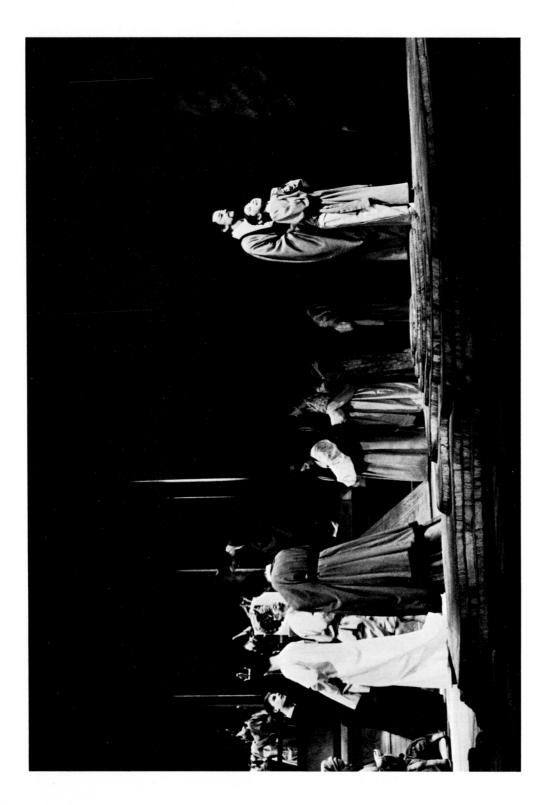

Throughout rehearsals, the director, stage manager, shop and technical people, and actors worked together to improve and refine each part of the play until all of the parts worked together smoothly. Every person worked on his or her own part so that it would fit with everyone else's parts. This is the method used in this theater to evolve an original work such as *The Nightingale* into the best possible production.

42

As parts of the sets were completed, rehearsals gradually took on the appearance of the final production.

The director was present at every rehearsal. In any play, the director is the person with the creative vision of what the final play should be. It is his or her job to see that these creative ideas are carried out onstage and that the different parts of the play focus, or come together, in a single story.

After each rehearsal, the director gave notes to the actors and stage crew on what he thought worked well and what he wanted changed.

44

A stage manager has an important job, too. He or she schedules when people are to appear onstage, when lighting, sound, and other special effects should come in, and also makes sure that all of the props are ready for each scene.

When the director ordered changes in any of these areas, the stage manager wrote them into her schedule and then instructed the crew and technical people in making the changes.

Finally the sets were nearly complete. Everyone in the cast had their lines memorized and their costumes and makeup finalized. It was time for preview night, a night when family and special friends of the theater people are invited to a test run of the finished play. A dress rehearsal was done earlier in the day, but now there would be a real audience.

Even on the day of the preview performance, last-minute work on the sets was still being done backstage. The designer

herself helped paint a flat, which would probably still be wet at that evening's performance.

At last it is time for the preview performance to begin. The house fills up with people. The lights grow dim. The curtain rises on the cast in the emperor's palace, and the people in the audience gasp at the beautiful scene.

All of the hard work done by the cast and all the people behind the scenes is rewarded by this sign that the theater has once again worked its magic.

48